Infused Readers

Book 1

American English Edition

Educational Solutions Worldwide Inc.

This book will introduce the sounds and spellings below.

These signs complete Words in Color Reading Primer R1, Table 1.

 t*a*p, p*a*n

 p*o*t, p*u*p*p*et

 *u*p, p*u*tt

 *t*an, pu*tt*

 *i*t, d*i*d

 a*s*, i*s*, dad'*s*

 p*e*n, s*e*nd

 *s*am, pa*ss*, it'*s*

 p*o*t, m*o*p

A note to educators & parents

This book follows the Words in Color approach to literacy, as invented by Dr. Caleb Gattegno. Our goal is to create independent learners who enjoy finding their own answers. Here are a few tips:

- Read the left-hand page, but don't read the right-hand page aloud.

- Ask questions such as, "Are you sure?" "Have you read this sound before?" and "What color was this sound?" rather than reading the difficult word and providing an example.

- Let the student try writing each sign after it is read in this book. Then say a sequence of sounds, and have the student write it. Then write some signs, and have the student read it. An example may be <u>auaa uuaa a u</u>. Check that the student reads the sounds with pauses where the spaces are, and writes the sounds with spaces where the pauses are. If they don't, ask them to read what you tap with a pencil (<u>auaa uuaa a u</u>). Try exaggerating the pause by tapping the sounds with a pencil, lifting the pencil up for the pause, then tapping again.

- Don't move on to the next sound until the student has mastered the previous one. Slowing down now will help accelerate the process in the long run.

- Refer to colors, not alphabet names. For example, this book introduces two sounds for the letter S. Rather than say "What sound does S make?" be more specific and say, "Is this the lime green sound, or the purple one? Read it like it's green. OK, try purple. Which is correct?"

- To further explore the sounds and signs, try using the Words in Color Word Charts, Reading Primers, and Workbooks. Many games and exercises can be found in *Teaching with Words in Color: Lesson Guides, Techniques, Games.*

a

This light pink sound is said *a* as in p*a*t.

Reading from left to right, read the sounds on the next page one at a time.

You can use your finger or a pointer to help follow along.

a   *a*

a

a   *a*   *a*   *a*

a   *a*

a   *a*   *a*   *a*

a   *a*

a

u

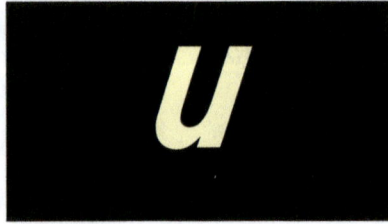

This light yellow sound is said u as in up.

Do you remember how to read a?

a　u　a　u

u

a　u

a　　u　　a　a　　a

a　a

a　a　u　a　a

a　　　　a

a

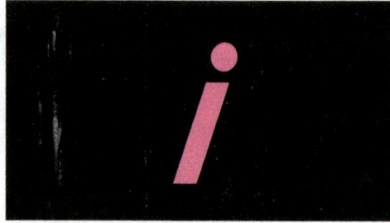

This hot pink sound is said *i* as in *i*t.

i   a i u u a u

        i u

        i   a u

a i u   a   a   a

        i   i   i a   a

        i   i

a i a u   a   i   a

a   i   a   i   i

        i   a   i   i   i

e

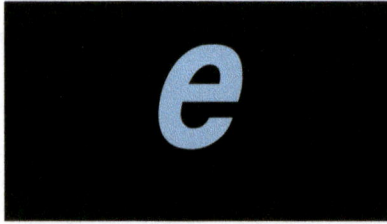

This blue sound is said e as in pet.

e   i   a i u   a u

  e   e i u   e

e   i   a u

a i u e a   a   e   a

  e   i   i   i a a   e

     i   i   e

a i a u e a i a   e

a   i   e   a i   i

     i   a   i i   i

  e

o

This white sound is said o̲ as in po̲t.

e i o a i u a u

o e e i u e o

e i o a u

a i u e a a e a

e i i i a a e

o i i e

a i a u e a i a e

a i e o a i i

o

o i a o i i o i

e

p

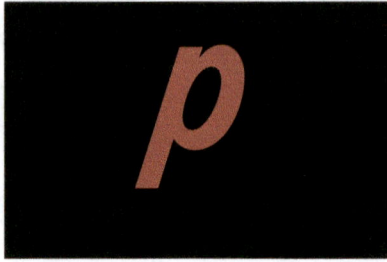

This reddish brown sound is said <u>together</u> with other sounds as in:

<u>p</u>at, <u>p</u>u<u>pp</u>y

When it looks like this

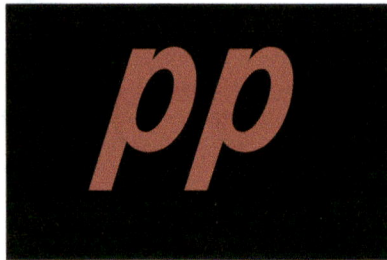

pp

we read it the same way.

e   ip pop pa i up pa u

pop e   e i up e   op

e   pi pop a u

pa i up e a pa   ep pa

e   pi   pi pi a pa   pe

po i   pi   e

pa i a up e a pi a e

a pi pe   po pa ip pi

pop

   op i pa   op i pi   op i

e

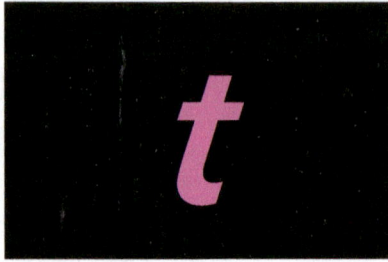

This dark pink sound is said together with other sounds as in:

t̲op, pu̲t̲t̲

When it looks like this

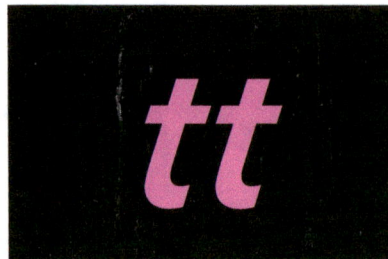

we read it the same way.

te   ip pop pat it up pa   u

pop te   et it up te   top

te   pit   pop at u

pat i   up et a   pat tep pa

te   pitt   pit   pit   at pat   pet

  pot it   pitt   te

pat i   a   up et at pitt a   te

a   pitt pet   pot pat tip   pitt

pop

  top it pat   top it pitt   top it

te

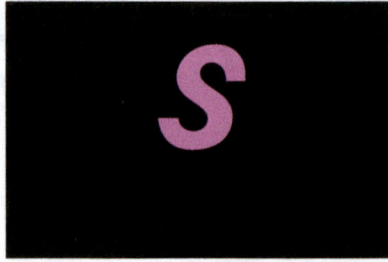

This purple sound is said together with other sounds as in:

i**s**, a**s**, wa**s**

te   ip pop pat it up pa   u

pop te   et it up te   top

te   pit pop at u

pat is up et as pat tep pa

te   pitt pit pit at pat   pet

 pot it   pitt   te

pat is as up et at pitt as te

as pitt pet   pot pat tip pitt

pop

  top it pat   top it pitt   top it

te

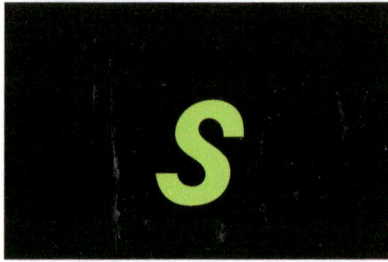

This lime green sound is said together with other sounds as in:

_s_am, pa_ss_, it'_s_

When it looks like this

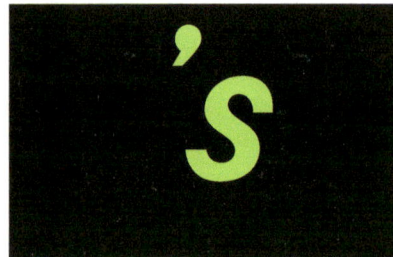

we read it the same way.

tess sips pop pat sits up pass us

pop tess set it up tess   stop

tess spits pop at us

pat is upset as pat steps past

tess pitt spits pits at pat's pet

spot it's pitt's test

pat is as upset at pitt as tess

as pitt pets spot pat tips pitt's

pop

stop it pat stop it pitt stop it

tess

tess sips pop. pat sits up. pass us pop tess. set it up. tess? stop! tess spits pop at us.

pat is upset. as pat steps past tess, pitt spits pits at pat's pet spot. it's pitt's test.

pat is as upset at pitt as tess. as pitt pets spot, pat tips pitt's pop.

stop it pat! stop it pitt! stop it tess!

pat	pots
pitt	pup
tess	pet
pass	pep
sit	pop
sat	as
spot	it
stop	is

pest	us
test	spat
steps	set
past	up
tap	sip
tip	top
pit	upset
putt	it's

step up pat. putt it.
stop! it's past us.

pat's sis tess putts it. it stops at
pop's steps.

pitt putts it up, up, up! it's past
pat's putt. pitt is upset.

step up pat. pat taps it. it tips!
pat's putt is tops.

For more information on learning to read, visit:

www.EducationalSolutions.com